SPEECH

OF

HON. DANIEL WEBSTER,

TO THE

YOUNG MEN OF ALBANY.

WEDNESDAY, MAY 28, 1851.

GIDEON & CO., Printers.

SPEECH

OF

HON. DANIEL WEBSTER,

TO THE

YOUNG MEN OF ALBANY.

WEDNESDAY, MAY 28, 1851.

GIDEON & Co., Printers.

INVITATION TO MR. WEBSTER.

On his journey from Buffalo to New York, Mr. WEBSTER received, before reaching Albany, the following letter of invitation, which he accepted :

To Hon. DANIEL WEBSTER :

SIR : The subscribers having learned that you will probably pass through our city early in the ensuing week, respectfully request an opportunity for our citizens generally, irrespective of party, and especially the young men of Albany, to testify their admiration of your character and talents as an American statesman, and their high appreciation of your public services in the councils of the nation.

They, therefore, respectfully invite you to partake with them of a dinner at Congress Hall, on the day of your arrival, or such other day as may suit your convenience.

They beg leave to add, that if your health will permit you to address our citizens at the Capitol, it would afford them great gratification to hear your views upon public affairs and the general condition of the country.

ALBANY, *May* 24, 1851.

Eli Perry,
John K. Porter,
William A. Rice,
James C. Kennedy,
B. R. Spelman,
James I. Johnson,
James Kidd,
Erastus Corning,
James H. Armsby,
James Hall,
Azor Taber,
T. Van Vechten, jr.,
Henry H. Martin,
R. S. Cushman,
Orlando Meads,
Abm. Van Vechten,
R. G. Beardslee,
L. Sprague Parsons,
Jerome Fuller,
R. L. Spelman,
Lewis Rathbone,
Isaac Edwards,
Erastus H. Pease,
Peter McNaughton,
Jacob C. Cuyler,
Ph. C. Fuller,
Chas. C. Miles,
John G. Erwin,
John I. Olmsted,
James McNaughton,
Thomas McElroy,
William Bay,
G. V. S. Bleecker,
John C. Spencer,
Watts Sherman,
Ezra P. Prentice,
John Townsend,
Teunis Van Vechten,
A. H. Root,
Thomas W. Olcott,
Samuel Stevens,
James D. Wasson,
Chas. S. Olmsted,
Archibald McClure,
Alexander Seward,
Charles M. Jenkins,
Gideon Hawley,
Lew. Benedict, jr.,
C. W. Goddard,
John McCardle,
David Wiltsie,
N. G. King,
Paul Cushman,
E. Satterlee,
Abm. F. Williams,
R. H. Waterman,
E. Henley,
A. W. Lee,
Richard Van Rensselaer,
J. S. Colt,
Jno. F. Rathbone,
S. H. Ransom,
Chris. Adams,
G. C. Davidson,
J. M. B. Davidson,
Stephen Van Rensselaer,

Theo. Townsend,
H. P. Pulling,
Samuel D. Vose,
H. Pumpelly,
Benj. Tibbits,
Cuyler Van Vechten,
E. E. Kendrick,
Lyman Chapin,
Henry Bleecker,
W. E. Bleecker,
John F. Townsend,
E. Wood,
Noah Lee,
Andrew McElroy,
C. Van Benthuysen,
John Newland,
Amos Dean,
R. H. Northrop,
George B. Steele,
Stephen Clark,
Rufus H. King,
Rufus W. Peckham,
Marcus T. Reynolds,
John Winne,
Alexander Marvin,
Alfred Stone,
James Edwards,
Lemuel Steele,
G. G. Hurll,
H. Davidson,
David Hamilton,
J. McNaughton,
Wm. Smith,
H. N. Dowd,
Townsend Fondey,
Thomas Olcott,
James Stevenson,
John D. Livingston,
H. Wyman,
James B. Sanders,
B. Sanders,
William Parmelee,
Samuel G. Courtney,
W. A. Young,
L. G. Bancroft,
P. Van Benthuysen,
J. N. Cutler,
John J. Olcott,
Wm. McElroy,
Andrew Kirk,
G. W. Peckham,
Maurice E. Viele,
W. L. Marcy,
Geo. C. Lee,
T. Romeyn Beck,
Wm. A. Corbiere,
R. V. Dewitt,
J. C. Feltman,
H. D. Stone,
J. Molinard,
Hale Kingsley,
Moses Patten,
Wm. W. Frothingham,
Silas B. Hamilton.

DEDICATION.

TO THE YOUNG MEN OF ALBANY:

THIS SPEECH, DELIVERED AT THEIR REQUEST, IS MOST RESPECTFULLY DEDICATED:

"COGITETIS OMNEM DIGNITATEM VESTRAM CUM REPUBLICA CONJUNCTAM ESSE DEBERE. UNA NAVIS EST JAM BONORUM OMNIUM; QUAM QUIDEM NOS DAMUS OPERAM, UT RECTAM TENEAMUS. UTINAM PROSPERO CURSU. SED QUICUNQUE VENTI ERUNT ARS NOSTRA CERTE NON ABERIT."

DAN'L WEBSTER.

SPEECH.

[At 2 o'clock in the afternoon of Wednesday, May 28th, Mr. WEBSTER was conducted by Messrs. PRICE and PORTER, of the Committee of Young Men, to the platform which had been erected near the Capitol; and having seated himself, cheers long and loud were given by the assembled multitude, which had been gathering for more than an hour, and now stood an immense mass, closely packed together.

The Hon. J. C. SPENCER announced that, at the request of the citizens of Albany, and especially the young men, the Hon. DANIEL WEBSTER had consented to address them on the present condition of the country and public affairs.

This announcement was received with renewed cheering.]

MR. WEBSTER rose and said:

FELLOW-CITIZENS: I owe the honor of this occasion, and I esteem it an uncommon and extraordinary honor, to the young men of this city of Albany, and it is my first duty to express to these young men my grateful thanks for the respect they have manifested towards me. Nevertheless, nevertheless, young men of Albany, I do not mistake you, or your object, or your purpose. I am proud to take to myself whatever may properly belong to me, as a token of personal and political regard from you to me. But I know, young men of Albany, it is not I, but the cause; it is not I, but your own generous attachments to your country; it is not I, but the Constitution of the Union, which has bound together your ancestors and mine, and all of us, for more than half a century. It is this that has brought you here to-day, to testify your regard toward one, who, to the best of his humble ability, has sustained that cause before the country. (Cheers.) Go on, young men of Albany! Go on, young men of the United States! Early manhood is the chief prop and support, the reliance and hope, for the preservation of public liberty and the institutions of the land. Early manhood is ingenuous, generous, just. It looks forward to a long life of honor or dishonor, and it means, by the blessing of God, that it shall be a life of honor, of usefulness, and success, in all the professions and pur suits of life, and that it shall close, when close it must, with some claim to the gratitude of the country. Go on, then; uphold the institutions to which you were born. You are manly and bold. You fear nothing but to do wrong; dread nothing but to be found recreant to patriotism and your country.

Gentlemen, I certainly had no expectation of appearing in such an assemblage as this to-day. It is not probable that, for a long time to come, I may again address any large meeting of my fellow-citizens. If I should not, and if this were the last, or to be among the last of all the occasions on which I am to appear before any great number of the people of the country, I shall not regret that that appearance was here. I find myself in the political capital of the greatest, most commercial, most powerful State of the Union. I find myself invited to be here by persons of the highest respectability, without distinction of party. I consider the occasion as somewhat august. I know that among those who now listen to me there are such as are of the wisest, the best, the most patriotic, and the most experienced public and private men in the State of New York. Here are governors and ex-governors, here are judges and ex-judges, of high character and high station; and here are persons from all the walks of professional and private life, distinguished for talent, and virtue, and eminence. Fellow-citizens, before such an assemblage, and on such an invitation, I feel bound to guard every opinion and every expression; to speak with precision such sentiments as I advance, and to be careful in all that I say, that I may not be misapprehended or misrepresented. I am requested, fellow-citizens, by those who invited me, to signify my sentiments on the state of public affairs in this country, and the interesting questions which are before us.

This proves, gentlemen, that in their opinion there are questions sometimes arising, which range above all party, and all the influences, and considerations, and interests of party. It proves more; it proves that, in their judgment, this is a time in which public affairs do rise in importance above the range of party, and draw to them an interest paramount to all party considerations. If that be not so, I am here without object, and you are listening to me for no purpose whatever.

Then, gentlemen, what is the condition of public affairs which makes it necessary and proper for men to meet, and confer together on the state of the country? What are the questions which are overriding, subduing, and overwhelming party, uniting honest, well meaning persons to lay party aside, to meet and confer for the general weal? I shall, of course, fellow-citizens, not enter at large into many of these questions, nor into any lengthened discussion of the state of public affairs, but shall endeavor to state what that condition is, what these questions are, and to pronounce a conscientious judgment of my own upon the whole.

The last Congress, fellow citizens, passed laws called adjustment measures, or settlement measures; laws intended to put an end to certain internal and domestic controversies which existed in the country, and some of which had existed for a long time. These laws were passed by the constitutional majorities of both houses of Congress. They received the constitutional approbation of the President. They are the laws of the land. To some, or all of them, indeed to all of them, at the time of their passage, there existed warm and violent opposition. None of them passed without heated discussion. Government was established in each of the territories of New Mexico and Utah, but not without opposition. The boundary of Texas was to be settled by compromise with that State, but not without determined and violent resistance. These laws all passed, however, and, as they have now become, from the nature of the case, irrepealable, it is not necessary that I should detain you by discussing their merits and demerits. Nevertheless, gentlemen, I desire on this and all public occasions, in the most emphatic and clear manner to declare, that I hold some of these laws, and especially that which provided for the adjustment of the controversy with Texas, to have been essential to the preservation of the public peace.

I will not now argue that point, nor lay before you at large the circumstances which existed at that time; the peculiar situation of things in so many of the Southern States; the fact that many of those States had adopted measures for the separation of the Union; or the fact that Texas was preparing to assert her rights to territory which New Mexico thought was hers by right, and that hundreds and thousands of men, tired of the ordinary pursuits of private life, were ready to rise and unite in any enterprise that might open itself to them, even at the risk of a direct conflict with the authority of this Government. I say, therefore, without going into the argument with any details, that in March of 1850, when I found it my duty to address Congress on these important topics, it was my conscientious belief, still unshaken, ever since confirmed, that if the controversy with Texas could not be amicably adjusted, there must, in all probability, have been civil war and civil bloodshed; and in the contemplation of such a prospect, it appeared of little consequence on which standard victory should perch; although, in such a contest, we took it for granted that no opposition could arise to the authority of the United States, that would not be suppressed. But what of that? I was not anxious about the military consequences of things; I looked to the civil and political state of things and their results, and I inquired what would be the condition of the country if, in this state of agitation, if, in this vastly extended, though not generally pervading feeling at the South, war should break out, and bloodshed should ensue in that extreme of the Union? That was enough for me to inquire into and regard; and, if the chances had been but one in a thousand that civil war would have been the result, I should still have felt that that one thousandth chance should be guarded against by any reasonable sacrifice, because, gentlemen, sanguine as I am for the future prosperity of the country; strongly as I believe now, after what has passed, and especially after those measures to which I have referred, that it is likely to hold together, I yet believe firmly that this Union, once broken, is utterly incapable, according to all human experience, of being re-constructed in its original character, of being re-cemented by any chemistry, or art, or effort, or skill of man. Now, gentlemen, let us pass from those measures which are now accomplished and settled. California is in the Union and cannot be got out; the Texas boundary is settled, and cannot be disturbed; Utah and New Mexico are territories, under provision of law, according to accustomed usage in former cases, and these things may be regarded as finally adjusted. But then there was another subject, equally agitating and equally irritating, which, in its nature, must always be subject to consideration or proposed amendment, and that is, the fugitive slave law of 1850, passed at the same session of Congress.

Allow me to advert, very shortly, to what I consider the ground of that law. You know, and I know, that it was very much opposed in the Northern States; sometimes with argument not unfair, often by mere ebullition of party, and often by those whirlwinds of fanaticism that raise a dust and blind the eyes, but produce no other effect. Now, gentlemen, this question of the propriety of the fugitive slave law, or the enactment of some such law, is a question that must be met. Its enemies will not let it sleep or slumber. They will "give neither sleep to their eyes nor slumber to their eyelids" so long as they can agitate it before the people. It is with them a topic, a desirable topic, and all know who have much experience in political affairs, that for party men, and in party times, there is hardly anything so desirable as a topic. (Laughter.) Now, gentlemen, I am ready to meet this question. I am ready to meet it, and ready to say that it was right, proper, expedient and just, that a suitable law should be passed for the restoration of fugitive slaves, found in free States, to their owners in slave States. I am ready to say that, because I only repeat the words of the Constitution itself, and I am not afraid of being considered a plagiarist, nor a feeble imitator of other men's language and sentiments, when I repeat and announce to every part of the country, to you, here, and at all times, the language of the Constitution of my country. (Loud cheers.) Gentlemen, before the Revolution, slavery existed in the Southern States, and had existed there, for more than a hundred years. We of the North were not guilty of its introduction. That generation of men, even in the South, were not guilty of it. It had been introduced according to the policy of the mother country, before there was any independence in the United States; indeed, before there were any authorities in the colonies competent to resist it. Why, gentlemen, men's opinions have so changed on this subject, and properly, the world has come to so much juster sentiments, that we can hardly believe, what is certainly true, that at the peace of Aix la Chapelle, in 1748, the English Government insisted on the fulfilment, to its full extent, of a condition in the treaty of the Assiento, signed at Utrecht, in 1713, by which the Spanish Government had granted the unqualified and exclusive privilege to the British Government of importing slaves into the Spanish colonies in America! That was not then repugnant to public sentiment; happily such a contract would be execrated now.

I allude to this, only to show, that the introduction of slavery into the Southern States is not to be visited upon the generation that achieved the Independence of this country. On the contrary, all the eminent men of that day regretted its existence. And you, my young friends of Albany, if you will take the pains to go back to the debates of the period, from the meeting of the first Congress in 1774, I mean the Congress of the Confederation, to the adoption of the present Constitution, and the enactment of the first law under the existing Constitution, you and anybody who will make that necessary research, will find that Southern men and Southern States, as represented in Congress, lamented the existence of slavery in far more earnest and emphatic terms than the Northern; for, though it did exist in the Northern States, it was a feeble taper, just going out, soon to end, and nothing was feared from it; while leading men of the South, of Virginia and the Carolinas, felt and acknowledged that it was a moral and political evil; that it weakened the arm of the freeman, and kept back the progress and success of free labor, and they said with truth, and all history verifies the observation, "that if the shores of the Chesapeake had been made as free to free labor as the shores of the North river, New York might have been great, but Virginia would have been great also." That was the sentiment.

Now, under this state of things, gentlemen, when the Constitution was framed, its framers, and the people who adopted it, came to a clear, express, unquestionable stipulation and compact. There had been an ancient practice, a practice for a century, for aught I know, according to which fugitives from service, whether apprentices at the North, or slaves at the South, should be restored. Massachusetts had restored fugitive slaves to Virginia long before the adoption of the Constitution, and it is well known that in other States, in which slavery did or did not exist, they were restored also, on proper application. And it was held that any man could pursue his slave and take him wherever he could find him. Under this state of things, it was expressly stipulated, in the plainest language, and there it stands; sophistry cannot gloss it, it cannot be erased from the page of the Constitution; there it stands; that persons held to service or labor in one State, under the laws thereof, escaping into another, shall not, in consequence of any law or regulation therein, be discharged from such service or labor, but shall be delivered up, upon claim of the party to whom such service or labor shall be due. This was adopted without dissent, nowhere objected to, north or south, but considered as a matter of absolute right and justice to the Southern States, concurred in everywhere, by every State that adopted the Constitution; and we look in vain for any opposition, from Massachusetts to Georgia.

Then, this being the case, this being the provision of the Constitution, it was found necessary, in General Washington's time, to pass a law to carry that provision of the Constitution into effect. Such a law was prepared and passed. It was prepared by a gentleman from a Northern State. It is said to have been drawn up by Mr. Cabot, of Massachusetts. It was supported by him, and by Mr. Goodhue, and by Mr. Sedgwick, of Massachusetts, and generally by all the free States. It passed without a division in the Senate, and with but seven votes against it in the House. It went into operation, and, for a time, it satisfied the just rights and expectations of everybody. That law provided that its enactments should be carried into effect mainly by State magistrates, justices of the peace, judges of State courts, sheriffs, and other organs of State authority. So things went on without loud complaints from any quarter, until some fifteen years ago, when some of the States, the free States, thought it proper for them to pass laws prohibiting their own magistrates and officers from executing this law of Congress, under heavy penalties, and refusing to the United States' authorities the use of their prisons for the detention of persons arrested as fugitive slaves. That is to say, these States passed acts defeating the law of Congress, as far as was in their power to defeat it. Those of them to which I refer, not all, but several, nullified the law of 1793 entirely. They said "We will not execute it. No runaway slave shall be restored." Thus the law became a dead letter, an entire dead letter. But here was the constitutional compact, nevertheless, still binding; here was the stipulation, as solemn as words could form it, and which every member of Congress, every officer of the General Government, every officer of the State governments, from governors down to constables, are sworn to support. Well, under this state of things, in 1850, I was of opinion that common justice and good faith called upon us to make a law, fair, reasonable, equitable and just, that should be calculated to carry this constitutional provision into effect, and give the Southern States what they were entitled to, and what it was intended originally they should receive, that is, a fair, right, and reasonable means to recover their fugitives from service from the States into which they had fled. I was of opinion that it was the bounden duty of Congress to pass such a law. The South insisted they had a right to it, and I thought they properly so insisted. It was no concession, no yielding of anything, no giving up of anything. When called on to fulfil a compact, the question is, will you fulfil it? And, for one, I was ready. I said, "I will fulfil it by any fair and reasonable act of legislation." Now, the law of 1850 had two objects, both of which were accomplished: First, it was to make the law more favorable for the fugitive than the law of 1793. It did so, because it called for a record, under seal, from a court in the State from which the fugitive came, proving and ascertaining that he was a fugitive, so that nothing should be left, when pursued into a free State, but to produce the proof of his identity. Next, it secured a higher tribunal, and it placed the power in more responsible hands. The judges of the Supreme and District Courts of the United States, and learned persons appointed by them as commissioners, were to see to the execution of the law. Therefore, it was a more favorable law, in all respects, to the fugitive, than the law passed under General Washington's administration in 1793. And the second object was to carry the constitutional provision into effect by the authority of law, seeing that the States had prevented the execution of the former law.

Now, let me say that this law has been discussed, considered, and adjudged in a great many of the tribunals of the country. It has been the subject of discussion before judges of the Supreme Court of the United States, the subject of discussion before courts the most respectable in the States. Everywhere, on all occasions, and by all judges, it has been holden to be, and pronounced to be, a constitutional law. So say Judges McLean, Nelson, Woodbury, and all the rest of the judges, as far as I know, on the bench of the Supreme Court of the United States. So says the unanimous opinion of Massachusetts herself, expressed by as good a court as ever sat in Massachusetts, its present supreme court, unanimously, and without hesitation. And so says everybody, eminent for learning, and constitutional law, and good judgment, without opposition, without intermixture of dissent, or difference of judicial opinion anywhere. And I hope I may be indulged on this occasion, gentlemen, partly on account of a high personal regard, and partly for the excellence and ability of the production, to refer you all to a recent very short opinion of Mr. Prentiss, the district judge of Vermont. (Applause.) True, the case before him did not turn so much on the question of the constitutionality of this law, as upon the unconstitutionality, and illegality, and utter inadmissibility, of the notion of private men and political bodies setting up their own whims, or their own opinions, above it, on the idea of the higher law that exists somewhere between us and the third heaven, I never knew exactly where. (Cries of "good," and laughter.)

All judicial opinions are in favor of this law. You cannot find a man in the profession in New York, whose income reaches thirty pounds a year, who will stake his professional reputation on an opinion against it. If he does, his reputation is not worth the thirty pounds. (Renewed laughter.) Aud yet this law is opposed, violently opposed, not by bringing this question into court: these lovers of human liberty, these friends of the slave, the fugitive slave, do not put their hands in their pockets and draw funds to conduct law suits, and try the question; they are not in that habit much. (Laughter.) That is not the way they show their devotion to liberty of any kind. But they meet and pass resolutions; they resolve that the law is oppressive, unjust, and should not be executed at any rate, or under any circumstances. It has been said in the States of New York, Massachusetts, and Ohio, over and over again, that the law shall not be executed. That was the language of a convention in Worcester, in Massachusetts; in Syracuse, New York, and elsewhere. And for this they pledged their lives, their fortunes, and their sacred honor! (Laughter.) Now, gentlemen, these proceedings, I say it upon my professional reputation, are distinctly treasonable. Resolutions passed in Ohio, certain resolutions in New York, and in the conventions held in Boston, are distinctly treasonable. And the act of taking away Shadrach from the public authorities in Boston, and sending him off, was an act of clear treason. I speak this in the hearing of men who are lawyers; I speak it out to the country; I say it everywhere, on my professional reputation. It was treason, and nothing less; that is to say, if men get together, and combine together, and resolve that they will oppose a law of the Government, not in any one case, but in all cases; I say if they resolve to resist the law, whoever may be attempted to be made the subject of it, and carry that purpose into effect, by resisting the application of the law in any one case, either by force of arms or force of numbers, that, sir, is treason. (Turning to Mr. Spencer, and stamping with emphasis.) You know it well. (Continuing to address Mr. Spencer.) The resolution, itself, unacted on, is not treason; it only manifests a treasonable purpose. When this purpose is proclaimed, and it is proclaimed that it will be carried out in all cases, and is carried into effect, by force of arms or numbers, in any one case, that constitutes a case of levying war against the Union; and if it were necessary, I might cite, in illustration, the case of John Fries, convicted in Washington's time, for being concerned in the whiskey insurrection in Pennsylvania. Now, various are the arguments, and various the efforts, to denounce this law; to oppose its execution; to keep it up as a question of agitation and popular excitement; and they are as diverse as the varied ingenuity of man, and the aspect of such questions when they come before the public. And a common thing it is to say that the law is odious; that therefore, it cannot be executed, and will not be executed. That has always been said by those who do not mean it shall be executed; not by anybody else. They assume the fact, that it cannot be executed, to make that true which they wish shall turn out to be true. They wish that it shall not be executed, and, therefore, announce to all mankind that it cannot be executed.

When public men, and the conductors of newspapers of influence and authority, thus deal with the subject, they deal unfairly with it. Those who have types at command, have a perfect right to express their opinions; but I doubt their right to express opinions as facts. I doubt whether they have a right to say, not as a matter of opinion, but of fact, that this particular law is so odious, here and elsewhere, that it cannot be executed. That only proves that they are of opinion that it ought not, that they hope it may not, be executed. They do not say, "See if any wrong is inflicted on anybody by it, before we wage war upon it; let us hope to find in its operation no wrong or injury to anybody. Let us give it a fair experiment." Do any of them hold that language? Not one. "The wish is father to the thought." They wish that it may not be executed, and therefore they say it cannot and will not be executed. That is one of the modes of presenting the case to the people; and, in my opinion, it is not quite a fair mode of doing it. There are other forms and modes; and I might omit to notice the blustering Abolition societies of Boston and elsewhere, as unworthy of regard; but there are other forms more insidious, and equally efficacious. There are men who say, when you talk of amending that law, that they hope it will not be touched. You talk of attempting it, and they dissuade you. They say, "Let it remain as obnoxious as it can be, and so much the sooner it will disgust, and be detested by, the whole community."

I am grieved to say that such sentiments have been avowed by those in Massachusetts who ought to be ashamed, utterly ashamed, to express such opinions. For, what do they mean ? They mean to make the law obnoxious; so obnoxious that it shall not be executed. But still they suggest no other law; they oppose all amendment; oppose doing anything that shall make it less distasteful. What do they mean ? They mean, and they know it, that there shall exist no law whatever for carrying into effect this provision of the Constitution of the country, if they can prevent it, let the consequences be what they may. They wish to strike out this constitutional provision; to annul it. They oppose it in every possible form short of personal resistance, or incurring personal danger; and to do this, they say the worse the law is the better. They say we have now a topic, and for mercy's sake don't amend the horrible law of 1850. (Laughter.) Then, again, they say, "We are for an eternal agitation and discussion of this question; the people cannot be bound by it. Every member of Congress has the right to move the repeal of this as well as any other law." Who does not know this, gentlemen ? A member must act according to his own discretion. No doubt he has a right to-morrow, if Congress were in session, to move a repeal of the Fugitive Slave Law; but this takes with it another consideration.

He has just as much right to move to tear down the Capitol, until one stone shall not be left on another; just as much right to move to disband the army, and to throw the ordnance and arms into the sea. He has just as much right to move that all the ships of war of the United States shall be collected and burned; an illumination like that which lit up the walls of ancient Troy. He may move to do any of these things. The question is, Is he prudent, wise; a real friend of the country, or adverse to it ? That is all. And a greater question lies behind : Will the people support him in it ? Is it the result of the good sense of the Northern people, that the question shall have neither rest nor quiet, but shall be constantly kept up as a topic of agitation ? I cannot decide this question for the people, but leave them to decide it for themselves. And now, gentlemen, this is a serious question, whether the Constitution can be maintained in part and not in whole ? Whether those interested in the preservation of one part of it, finding their interests in that particular abandoned, are not likely enough, according to all experience of human feeling and human conduct, to discard that portion which was introduced, not for their benefit, but for the benefit of others ? That is the question. For one, I confess, I do not see any reasonable prospect of maintaining the Constitution of the United States, unless we maintain it as a whole; impartially, honorably, patriotically. Gentlemen, I am detaining you too long; but allow me a few words on another subject, by way of illustration.

The Constitution of the United States consists in a series of mutual agreements or compromises, one thing being yielded by the South, another by the North; the general mind having been brought together, and the whole agreed to, as I have said, as a series of compromises constituting one whole. Well, gentlemen, who does not see that? Had the North, no particular interest to be regarded and protected? Had the North no peculiar interest of its own? Was nothing yielded by the South to the North? Gentlemen, you are proud citizens of a great commercial State. You know that New York ships float over the whole world, and bring abundance of riches to your own shores. You know that this is the result of the commercial policy of the United States, and of the commercial power vested in Congress by the Constitution. And how was this commerce established? by what constitutional provisions, and for whose benefit? The South was never a commercial country. The plantation States were never commercial. Their interest always was, as they thought, what they think it to be now, free trade, the unrestricted admission of foreigners in competition in all branches of business with our own people. But what did they do? They agreed to form a Government that should regulate commerce according to the wants and wishes of the Northern States, and when the Constitution went into operation, a commercial system was actually established, on which has risen up the whole glory of New York and New England. (Applause.)

Well, what did Congress do under a Northern lead with Southern acquiescence? What did it do? It protected the commerce of New York and the eastern States, by preference, by a way of tonnage duties; and that higher tonnage on foreign ships has never been surrendered to this day, but in consideration of a just equivalent; so, in that respect, without grudging or complaint on the part of the South, but generously and fairly, not by way of concession, but in the true spirit of the Constitution, the commerce of New York and the New England States was protected by the provision of the Constitution to which I have referred. But that is not all.

Friends! Fellow-citizens! Men of New York! Does this country not now extend from Maine to Mexico, and beyond? And have we not a State beyond Cape Horn, belonging nevertheless to us as part of our commercial system? And what does New York enjoy? What do Massachusetts and Maine enjoy? They enjoy an exclusive right of carrying on the coasting trade from to State to State, on the Atlantic and around Cape Horn to the Pacific. And that is a most highly important branch of business, and source of wealth and emolument, of comfort and good living. Every man must know this, who is not blinded by passion or fanaticism. It is this exclusive right to the coasting trade which the Northern States possess, which was granted to them, which they have ever held, and which, up to this day, there has been no attempt to rescue from them; it is this which has employed so much tonnage and so many men, and given support to so many thousands of our fellow-citizens. Now, what would you say, in this day of the prevalence of notions of free trade, what would you say, if the South and the West were to join together to repeal this law? And they have the votes to do it to-morrow. What would you say if they should join hands and resolve that these men of the North and New England, who put this slight on our interest, shall enjoy this exclusive privilege no longer? That they will throw it all open, and invite the Dane, the Swede, the Hamburger, and all the commercial nations of Europe who can carry cheaper, to come in and carry goods from New York coastwise on the Atlantic, and to California on the Pacific? What do you say to that?

Now, gentlemen, these ideas have been a thousand times suggested, perhaps, but if there is anything new in them, I hope it may be regarded. But what was said in Syracuse and Boston; it was this: "You set up profit against conscience; you set up the means of living; we go for conscience." (Laughter.) That is a flight of fanaticism. All I have to answer is, that if what we propose is right, fair, just, and stands well with a conscience not enlightened with those high flights of fancy, it is none the worse for being profitable; and that it does not make a thing bad which is good in itself, that you and I can live on it, and our children be supported and educated by it. If the compact of the Constitution is fair, and was fairly entered into, it is none the worse, one should think, for its having been found useful. (Renewed applause.) Gentlemen, I believe, in Cromwell's time, for I am not very fresh in my recollections of that historic period, I have had more to do with other things than some of you younger men that love to look into the instructive history of that age, but I think it was in Cromwell's time, that there sprang up a race of saints who called themselves "fifth monarchy men;" and a happy, felicitous, glorious people they were; for they had practised so many virtues, they were so enlightened, so perfect, that they got to be, in the language of that day, "above ordinances." That is the higher law of this day exactly. (Laughter.) Our higher law is but the old doctrine of the fifth monarchy men, of Cromwell's time, revived. They were above ordinances, walked about firm and spruce, self-satisfied, thankful to God that they were not as other men, but had attained so far to salvation as to be "above all necessity of restraint or control, civil or religious." (Renewed laughter.) Cromwell himself says of these persons, if I remember rightly, "that *notions* will hurt none but those that have them; but when they tell us, not that law is to regulate us, but that law is to be abrogated and subverted, and perhaps the Judaical law brought in, instead of our own laws settled among us," this is something more than a notion, "this is worthy of every magistrate's consideration."

Gentlemen, we live under a Constitution. It has made us what we are. What has carried the American flag all over the world ? What has constituted that unit of commerce, that wherever the stars and stripes are seen, they signify that it is America and united America ? What is it now that represents us so respectably all over Europe ? in London at this moment, and all over the world? What is it but the result of those commercial regulations which united us all together, and made our commerce, the same commerce; which made all the States, New York, Massachusetts, South Carolina, in the aspect of our foreign relations, the same country, without division, distinction, or separation ? Now, gentlemen, this was the original design of the Constitution. We, in our day, must see to it; and it will be equally incumbent on you, my young friends of Albany, to see that while you live, this spirit is made to pervade the whole administration of the Government. The Constitution of the United States, to keep us united, to keep a fraternal feeling flowing in our hearts, must be administered in the spirit in which it was framed. And if I were to exhibit the spirit of the Constitution in its living, speaking, animated form, I would refer always, always, to the administration of the first President, George Washington. (Vehement cheering.) And if I were now to describe a patriot President, I would draw his master-strokes and copy his design ; I would present his picture before me as a constant study ; I would present his policy, alike liberal, just, narrowed down to no sectional interests, bound to no personal objects, held to no locality, but broad, and generous, and open, as expansive as the air which is wafted by the winds of heaven from one part of the country to another. (Cheers.)

I would draw a picture of his foreign policy, just, steady, stately, but withal proud, and lofty, and glorious. No man could say, in his day, that the broad escutcheon of the honor of the Union could receive injury or damage, or even contumely or disrespect, with impunity. His own character gave character to the foreign relations of the country. He upheld every interest of the United States in even the proudest nations of Europe; and while resolutely just, he was resolutely determined that no plume in the honor of the country should ever be defaced or taken from its proper position by any power on earth. Washington was cautious and prudent; no self-seeker; giving information to Congress, according to the Constitution, on all questions, when necessary, with fairness and frankness, claiming nothing for himself, exercising his own rights, and preserving the dignity of his station, but taking especial care to execute the laws as a paramount duty, and in such manner as to give satisfaction to all just and reasonable men. And it was always remarked of his administration, that he filled the courts of justice with the most spotless integrity, the highest talent, and the purest virtue; and hence it became a common saying, running through all classes of society, that our great security is in the learning and integrity of the judicial tribunals. This high character they justly possessed, and continue to possess in an eminent degree from the impress which Washington stamped on these tribunanls at their first organization.

Gentlemen, a patriot President of the United States is the guardian, the protector, the friend of every citizen in them. He should be, and he is, no man's persecutor, no man's enemy, but the supporter and the protector of all and every citizen, so far as such support and protection depend on his faithful execution of the laws. But there is especially one great idea which Washington presents, and which governed him, and which should govern every man in high office, who means to resemble Washington: that is, the duty of preserving the Government itself; of suffering, so far as depends on him, no one branch to interfere with another, and no power to be assumed not belonging to each, and none abandoned which pertains to each; but to preserve it and carry it on unharmed for the benefit of the present and future generation.

Gentlemen, a wise and prudent shipmaster makes it his first duty to preserve the vessel which carries him, and his passengers, and all that is committed to his charge; to keep her afloat, to conduct her to her destined port with entire security of property and life; that is his first object, and that should be the object, and is, of every Chief Magistrate of the United States, who has a proper appreciation of his duty. His first and highest duty is to preserve the Constitution which bears him, which sustains the Government, without which every thing goes to the bottom; to preserve that, and keep it, with the utmost of his ability and foresight, off the rocks and shoals, and away from the quick-sands; to accomplish this great end, he exercises the caution of the experienced navigator. He suffers nothing to betray his watchfulness, or to draw him aside from the great interest committed to his care; but is always awake, always solicitous, always anxious, for the safety of the ship which is to carry him through the stormy seas.

> "Though pleased to see the dolphins play,
> He minds his compass and his way;
> And oft he throws the wary lead,
> To see what dangers may be hid:
> At helm he makes his reason sit,
> His crew of passions all submit.
> Thus, thus he steers his barque, and sails,
> On upright keel, to meet the gales!"

Now, gentlemen, a patriot President, acting from the impulses of this high and honorable purpose, may reach what Washington reached. He may contribute to raise high the public prosperity, to help to fill up the measure of his country's glory and renown; and he may be able to find a rich reward in the thankfulness of the people,

> "And read his history in a nation's eyes."

MR. SPENCER'S SPEECH

AT THE

DINNER GIVEN TO MR. WEBSTER, AT ALBANY, WEDNESDAY EVENING.

Mr. SPENCER rose and addressed the company as follows:

I am about to offer a sentiment, my friends, which you expect from the chair. The presence of the distinguished guest whom we have met to honor, imposes restraints which may not be overleaped. Within those limits, and without offending the generous spirit which has on this occasion discarded all political and partisan feeling, I may recall to our recollections a few incidents in his public life, which have won for him the proud title of "Defender of the Constitution." (Great applause.)

When in 1832–'33, South Carolina raised her paricidal arm against our common mother, and the administration of the Government was in the hands of that man of determined purpose and iron will, Andrew Jackson, whose greatest glory was his inflexible resolution to sustain the Union or perish with it, (here the speaker was interrupted by deafening shouts of applause,) in that dark and gloomy day, where was our guest found? Did he think of paltry politics, of how much his party might gain by leaving their antagonists to fight the battle of the Union between themselves, and thus become a prey to their watchful opponents? No, gentlemen; you know what he did. He rallied his mighty energies, and tendered them openly and heartily to a political chieftain whose administration he had constantly opposed. (Cheers upon cheers.) He breasted himself to the storm. Where blows were thickest and heaviest, there was he; and when he encountered the great champion of the South, Colonel Hayne, in that immortal, intellectual struggle, the parallel of which no country has witnessed; the hopes, the breathless anxiety of a nation, hung upon his efforts; and, oh, what a shout of joy and gratulation ascended to heaven, at the matchless victory which he achieved. (Here, for some time, the speaker was unable to proceed, in consequence of the incessant and tumultuous cheering of the company, who had spontaneously risen from their seats.) Had he then been called to his fathers, the measure of his fame would have been full to overflowing, and he would have left a monument in the grateful recollection of his countrymen, such as no statesman of modern times had reared. (Renewed applause.) But he was reserved by a kind Providence for greater efforts. For more than twenty years, in the Senate Chamber, in the courts of justice, and in the executive councils, he has stood sentinel over the Constitution. It seems to have been the master passion of his life to love, to venerate, to defend, to fight for the Constitution, at all times and in all places. (Cheers upon cheers.) He did so because the Union existed and can exist only in the Constitution; and the peace and happiness of the country can exist only in the Union. In fighting for the Constitution, he fought therefore for the country, for the whole country.

I may not speak in detail of the many acts of his public life which have developed this absorbing love of country. But there are a few of the precious gems in the circlet which adorns his brow, that are so marked and prominent that they cannot be overlooked.

When he first assumed the duties of the Department of State, war was lowering on our horizon like a black cloud, ready to launch its thunderbolts around us. The alarming state of our foreign relations, at that time, is shown by the extraordinary fact that the appropriation bills passed by Congress, at the close of Mr. Van Buren's administration, contained an unusual provision, authorizing the President to transfer them to military purposes. In a few months after our guest took the matter in hand, the celebrated treaty with Lord Ashburton was concluded, by which the irritating question of boundary was settled, every difficulty then known or anticipated was adjusted, and among others, the detestable claim to search our vessels for British seamen was renounced.

In connexion with this treaty, I take this occasion, the first that has presented itself, to state some facts which are not generally known. The then administration had no strength in Congress; it could command no support for any of its measures. This was an obstacle sufficiently formidable in itself. But Mr. Webster had to deal with a feeble and wayward President, an unfriendly Senate, a hostile House of Representatives, and an accomplished British diplomatist. I speak of what I personally know, when I say, that never was a negotiation environed with greater or more perplexing difficulties. He had at least three parties to negotiate with instead of one, to say nothing of Massachusetts and Maine, who had to be consulted in relation to a boundary that affected their territory.* You

* For the purpose of explanation it may be well to say, that the Northeastern Boundary having been a matter of controversy for fifty years, and the award of the King of the Netherlands having finally failed, Mr. Webster proposed that a line should be established by agreement, upon the principle of fair equivalents, to be assented to by Massachusetts and Maine; accordingly Massachusetts appointed three commissioners and Maine four, selected from both political parties, to proceed to Washington, and take part in the negotiations. The consent of all the commissioners was made the condition of binding their respective States. It will thus be seen that the difficulty of making a treaty, when so many and such diverse interests were to be harmonized, was immeasurably increased.

know the result; glorious as it was to our country, how glorious was it also to the pilot that guided the ship through such difficulties! (Prolonged cheering.)

You have not forgotten how the generous sympathies of our guest were awakened in behalf of the noble Hungarians, in their immortal resistance against the force of barbarism. And sure I am there is not a heart here that has not treasured up the contents of that world-renowned letter to Chevalier Hülsemann, in answer to the intimations of threats by Austria to treat our diplomatic agent as a spy! What American was not proud of being the countryman of the author of that letter? (Cheers upon cheers silenced the speaker for some time.)

I confess I cannot now think of that letter without recollecting the sensations a particular part of it produced upon my risible faculties. I mean the comparison between the territories and national importance of the House of Hapsburgh and those of the United States of America. (A universal shout of merriment here interrupted the speaker again and again, and prevented him from proceeding for some time.)

But I must stop the enumeration of the great deeds in the glory of which we all participate, and by the results of which the whole civilized world has been benefitted. I must stop, or the setting sun would leave me still at the task, and the rising sun would find it unfinished.

The same soul-absorbing devotion to the country and to the Constitution, as its anchor of safety, has been exhibited so recently and so remarkably, that no one can have forgotten it. In the view which I present of the matter, it is quite immaterial whether we regard our guest as having been right or wrong. He deemed the course he took to be the only one permitted to him by his sense of duty. On the other side were the strong feelings with which, as a Northern man, he had always sympathized; there also were the friends of his youth and of his age; the troops of ardent and devoted admirers; all whose love was equal to their reverence; all the associations and affections of life were clustered there; while on the other side a feeling of enmity, engendered by former contests and the defeat of all their schemes, nothing to allure or invite, but every thing to repel except one, and that was the Constitution of the country; that, as he conscientiously believed, required him to interpose and prevent a breach of faith, as well as of the organic law, and avert a civil war that he believed was impending. He hesitated not a moment, but at once marched up to the deadly breach, and was ready to sacrifice upon his country's altar, more than life, every thing that could render life worth retaining.

My friends, whatever other view may be taken of that step, every one knows that it conformed to the whole plan of his public life to know no North, no South, where the Constitution was in question; and there is not a heart in this assembly that will not respond to my voice when I pronounce it heroism; heroism of the most sublime order. It can be compared only to that of the Great Reformer who, when advised not to proceed to the Diet that was convoked to condemn him, declared that if fifty thousand legions of devils stood in the way, go he would! (Prolonged and universal shouts.)

How poor and insignificant are all our efforts to express our appreciation of such a character and of such services. They have sunk deep in our hearts; they will sink deeper still in the hearts of the unborn millions who are to people this vast continent; and when he and we sleep with our fathers, his name will reverberate from the Atlantic to the Pacific, as the defender of the Constitution and of his country.

Gentlemen, I give you a sentiment which I think will be drank in bumpers and standing. (The whole assembly rose at once with acclamation:)

"THE CONSTITUTION OF THE UNITED STATES, AND DANIEL WEBSTER, INSEPARABLE NOW, AND INSEPARABLE IN THE RECORDS OF TIME AND ETERNITY."

Mr. WEBSTER rose to respond, and the whole company started from their seats, and gave him three times three cheers. Mr. W. said:

I know, gentlemen, very well how much of the undeserved compliment, or I may say eulogy, which you have heard from my honorable friend at the head of the table, is due to a personal and political friendship, which has now continued for many years; of course, I cannot but most profoundly thank him for the manner in which he has expressed himself. Gentleman, what shall *I* say? What shall *I* say to this outpouring of kindness? I am overwhelmed. I have no words. I cannot acknowledge the truth of what has been said, yet I hardly could find it in my heart to deny it. [Loud cheering.] It is overstated. It is overstated. But, that I love the Constitution of the country; that I have a passion for it, the only political passion that ever entered into my breast; that I cherish it day and night; that I live on its healthful, saving influences, and that I trust never, never, never, to cease to heed it till I go to the grave of my fathers, is as true as you sit here. [Turning to Mr. Spencer.] [Cheers, long and loud.] I do not suppose I am born to any considerable destiny, [cheers and laughter,] but my destiny attaches me to the Constitution of the country. I desire not to outlive it. I desire to render it some service. And, on the modest stone that shall mark my grave, whether within my native New Hampshire, or my adopted Massachusetts, I wish no other epitaph than this: while he lived, he did what he could to support the Constitution of his country. [Renewed cheering.] I confess to you that as to mere questions of politics, of expediency, I take my share in them, as they have gone along, in the course of my political life, which is now fast running through. But I have felt no anxiety, no excitement; nothing has made me lie awake at night, when it is said honest men sleep, except something that concerned the preservation of the Union! The Constitution of the United States! What is there on the whole earth; what is there that so fills the imaginations of men under heaven; what is there that the civilized, liberalized, liberty loving people of the world can look at, and do look at, so much as that great and glorious instrument, holden up to their contemplation, blazing over this western hemisphere, and darting its rays throughout the world, the Constitution of the United States of America! [Vehement cheering.] In Massachusetts, in New York, in Washington, its ample folds are athwart the whole heavens; are they not seen in all America, on all the continent of Europe, gazed at and honored in Russia, in Turkey, in the Indian seas, in all the countries of the oriental world?

[Cheers.] What is it that makes you and I here, to-day, so proud as we are of the name of America? What is it? It is a miracle; the achievement of half a century, by wise men under propitious circumstances, acting from patriotic motives; a miracle achieved on earth and in view of all nations; the establishing of a Government, taking hold on a great continent; covering ample space for fifty other governments; having 25,000,000 of people, intelligent, prosperous, brave, able to defend themselves against united mankind, and to bid defiance to the whole of them; a noble monument of republican honor and power, and of republican success, that throws a shade, and sometimes a deep and black shade, over the monarchies, and aristocracies, and despotisms of Europe. [Cheers.] Who is there, who is there from the poles to the Mediterranean, despot, aristocrat, autocrat, who is there that now dares to speak reproachfully or in tonesof derogation of the Government of the United States of America? [Cheers.] There is not one. And if we may judge, my friends, of the success of our system of government, from the regard it attracts from all nations, we may flatter ourselves that in our primitive republicanism, in our representative system, in our departure from the whole feudal code, and all the peculiarities of aristocratic and autocratic power, from all the show and pageantry of courts, we shall hold ourselves up like the face of the sun, not marred by inscriptions, but bright in glory, and glittering in the sight of all men. [Cheers.] And so we will stand, so shine, and when the time comes when I shall be gathered to my fathers, and you to yours, that eternal, unfading sun of American Liberty and Republicanism, as steady in its course as the sun in the heavens, shall still pour forth its beams for the enlightenment of mankind. [Vociferous applause.]

Gentlemen, I again thank you for the manner in which you have been pleased to receive the sentiment complimentary to me by my friend. I thank you, thank him. Gentlemen, I am happy to be here, in this ancient city. Of course, I like to see my Yankee brethren here, and a great many of them. [Laughter; a voice, "we have a codfish and pumpkin down here."] I have no objection to see the recent importations, so to describe them, come from where they may; because I am of opinion, and have expressed it again and again, that we have got to that stage in our affairs, that the world has reached that point in the system of change and innovation, that we are brought to this, that we have nothing to do but say to the inhabitants of the ancient world, the Irish, the Welch, the German, gentlemen, come; and the fact is, the cry is still they come. [Laughter and applause.] There are people enough imported into New York, twice a year, to make a city as large as old Salem or Naumkeag in Massachusetts. Every big ship brings them to our shores, and off they start to Wisconsin. Well, they come, and whether they come from Dublin, Cork, or Kerry, they are very happy to stay where they are. If they come from the north of Ireland, if they have a little of the canny Scotch in them, [the rest of this sentence was lost to the Reporter, from the noise in the street.] Every steamboat brings them, and every packet; and when you think they are all here, the cry is "still they come." Well, we must meet this as well as we can. Very many of them are excellent persons. [Much that Mr. W. said in continuation on this head, was lost to the Reporter.] I, continued Mr. Webster, am a New England man. I am of the Anglo-Saxon race; but it is my good fortune to be connected with a lady in life who has a little touch of the old Knickerbocker. [Laughter.] I am happy to know that among this company there are many persons of Dutch descent. I honor them all, and I accord to them credit for honesty, for sobriety of character, and for the great aid they have lent to the progress of population and prosperity in this and neighboring States.

[Mr. Webster here passed to the subject of the Union and its defence.] With my dying breath, (said he,) if I have my senses, my last prayer shall be, Heaven save my country and Government. I hear the cry of disunion, secession. The secession of individual States, to my mind, is the most absurd of all ideas. I should like to know how South Carolina is to get out of this Union. Where is she to go? [Laughter and cheers.] The commercial people of Charleston say, with truth and propriety, if South Carolina secedes from the Union, we secede from South Carolina. [Renewed laughter.] The thing is absurd. A separate secession is an absurdity. It could not take place. It must lead to war. But, then, I do admit the possibility that a great mass of the southern States, if they should come so far north as to include Virginia, might make a southern confederation. But it would put Virginia up to all she knows to accomplish it. [Laughter.] Because more than half of Virginia lies on the west slope of the Alleghanies, and is connected with the valley of the Mississippi, its people and interests, rather than with those who live on tide water. Do they think that the great western slope of the Alleghanies is to be included in a secession movement? Nevertheless it is a most serious consideration. All know what would be the result of any dismemberment of this Union, large or small. The philosophic poet tells us that in the frame of things above us, beneath us, and around us, there are connexions, mutual dependencies and relations, which link them together in one great chain of existencies, beginning from the throne on high, and running down to the lowest order of beings. There seems to be some analogy to this with our association here as separate States; independent yet connected; revolving in separate spheres, and yet mutually bound one with another. And what he poet says of the great chain that holds all together in the moral, in-ellectual, and physical world, is applicable to this chain of States,

> ——whatever link you strike,
> Tenth, or ten thousandth, breaks the chain alike.

[This sentiment drew out long continued cheering.]

Now, gentlemen, it is not for me to do much more, nor attempt much more, on this theatre of action. I look on to see what others shall do, and to see what the rising generation shall do. I look on to see what the young men of the country are determined to do. I see them intelligent, regardless of personal objects, holding on upon what their ancestors gave them, holding on with their whole strength to the institutions of the country. I know that when I shall slumber in the dust, the institutions of the country will be free and safe; I know that the young men of the country can preserve the country. In the language of the old Greek orator, "the young are the spring-time of the people." I wish to leave my exhortation to the young men all over the country; to say to them, on you, young men of the Republic, the hopes, the independence, the Union, the honor of the country, entirely depend. May God bless you. In taking leave of you, whilst I shall never forget the pleasure this occasion has given me, I give you as a sentiment:

"THE YOUNG MEN OF ALBANY, THE YOUNG MEN OF THIS GENERATION, AND OF THE SUCCEEDING GENERATIONS—MAY THEY LIVE FOREVER, BUT MAY THE CONSTITUTION AND THE UNION OUTLIVE THEM ALL."

Cheer upon cheer followed the reading of this sentiment, and the Band struck up the "Star Spangled Banner."

www.ingramcontent.com/pod-product-compliance
Lightning Source LLC
LaVergne TN
LVHW011133110826
845150LV00008B/2321

* 9 7 8 1 4 1 8 1 9 4 7 8 9 *